Koudama Zeroual

Innovation in Takaful Insurance

**Koudama Zeroual**

# Innovation in Takaful Insurance

**ScienciaScripts**

**Imprint**

Any brand names and product names mentioned in this book are subject to trademark, brand or patent protection and are trademarks or registered trademarks of their respective holders. The use of brand names, product names, common names, trade names, product descriptions etc. even without a particular marking in this work is in no way to be construed to mean that such names may be regarded as unrestricted in respect of trademark and brand protection legislation and could thus be used by anyone.

Cover image: www.ingimage.com

This book is a translation from the original published under ISBN 978-620-2-28045-7.

Publisher:
Sciencia Scripts
is a trademark of
Dodo Books Indian Ocean Ltd. and OmniScriptum S.R.L publishing group

120 High Road, East Finchley, London, N2 9ED, United Kingdom
Str. Armeneasca 28/1, office 1, Chisinau MD-2012, Republic of Moldova, Europe
Printed at: see last page
ISBN: 978-620-5-85473-0

# SUMMARY

# SYNTHESIS

Unlike conventional finance, the success of Islamic finance depends on both faith and economics.

Furthermore, it is important to remember that the goal of Takaful practitioners is not to systematically "replicate" the products and services of conventional insurance in accordance with Islamic percepts, but to create new products and services that meet the needs of policyholders, even if this sometimes means slower growth. The challenge is to overcome the image of "cosmetic accounting" that unduly sticks to the Takaful business.

Innovation must address products and services, processes and distribution.

Until now, the insurance industry has always been able to renew its approaches and models and adapt its offers to societal changes. Today, almost all of this activity is being re-questioned, all the more so as it is being traversed, like other financial activities, by the digital revolution.

Will the insurance industry, and particularly Takaful, be able to adapt? And above all, will they be able to impose themselves before others take their place?

The installation and implementation of new Takaful companies in Morocco is an opportunity to build the business on new innovative approaches.

The digital path is strongly indicated in a process of innovation affecting the customer approach, the customer experience and risk modeling; while integrating fintechs, particularly insurtechs, into the "product" thinking in order to channel them and make them their own.

# INTRODUCTION:

Islamic finance is considered a stable financial system that promotes growth and equity. It is considered more responsible by its perfect connection with the real economy and by excluding interest, speculation, hoarding and uncertainty in contracts.

Islamic finance conveys universal moral and ethical principles. It has demonstrated through its various compartments (banks, insurance, capital market ...) a dynamism, resilience and resistance to the latest financial and economic turbulence that the world has experienced.

However, research and literature on this finance is scarce and inaccessible, and even if it is accessible, it is focused on religious and Sharia aspects,

Islamic finance is often criticized for being close to and imitating the conventional model. There are of course some areas where it is not necessary to reinvent oneself.

Takaful is essentially insurance, providing financial protection. It remains based on the indemnity principle to financially compensate for losses and damages caused by unforeseen risks, just like conventional insurance.

It is based on scientific rules, actuarial approaches and management rules that are similar or even identical to those of conventional insurance.

In fact, the existing technical aspect of the insurance is the same base with some adjustments.

It is not a matter of rethinking or re-doing things differently to be different, but using the existing acceptable as a leverage to achieve the purpose of the Takaful principles.

These principles provide a strong ethic to risk management, application of actuarial and mathematical techniques, mutuality in the use of money for the benefit of the community of participants, improved performance of the insurance enterprise, sustained growth and preservation of the environment.

Innovation, on the other hand, which will be defined in the first part, can be a revolution or an evolution. If Takaful is qualified as an innovation in the field of insurance, this innovation brings a revolutionary change in the management, investment and distribution of money as well as in the sharing of risks. Evolutionary innovation is manifested in products and services.

The first part will focus on some definitions and concepts: Takaful and its evolution, the concept of innovation. The second part of the presentation will focus on innovation in Takaful, and will look at how Takaful is innovating in Morocco, with a focus on digital technology, a privileged way to differentiate in the Moroccan sector. And finally the limits and challenges of innovation in Takaful.

# Part I: INNOVATION IN TAKAFUL

*"...innovation must always be easy to understand, to exploit. The limit of innovation is understanding."*

Thomas Kroely, Divisional Director of Willis Re

*"A phenomenon, idea, or paradigm that helps create a new market with a value system and eventually disrupts an existing market by changing the status quo is a standard definition of disruptive innovation. Takaful is a disruptive innovation."*

**Takaful and Islamic Cooperative Finance: Challenges and Opportunities**

Published by S. Nazim Ali, Shariq Nisar

## 1.1. TAKAFUL:

Before defining Takaful, which in itself is a form of insurance. A reminder of the principle of insurance is necessary.

### 1.1.1. INSURANCE

Insurance is an operation by which a party (the insurer) undertakes to provide a service, within the framework of an insurance contract, for the benefit of another individual (the insured) in the event of the occurrence of a risk, in return for a remuneration, the payment of a contribution or a premium.

The risk is the object of the insurance. An insured takes out insurance to protect himself against harmful events (illness, fire, theft, death, etc.) or against risks related to certain objects in his estate (home, car) or related to his activity or responsibilities (employees, machinery, etc.).

In the event of a risk, the insurer is obliged to pay a benefit in the form of money either to the insured, a third party or, in the case of life insurance, to the beneficiary. In return for this benefit, the insured pays a premium or contribution to the insurer. This sum corresponds to the cost of the risk and the insurer's operating expenses.

## 1.1.2. THE TAKAFUL

Takaful is the Islamic concept of insurance, it comes from the verb "KAFALA", which means "to guarantee each other" or "joint guarantee". The Takaful system is based on mutual cooperation, responsibility, insurance, protection and assistance between groups of participants.

Takaful is not only for Muslim policyholders, it is an "ethical" alternative to conventional insurance. This is not to say that Takaful has a monopoly on ethics or that it is specifically dedicated to Muslim policyholders. Indeed, Islamic ethics are based on values of responsibility, social justice, sharing, mutuality and balance, which are quite universalizable.

Takaful insurance does not involve the rules of religious rituals, but those of economic and social relationships, the term Takaful simply meaning "to guarantee one another".

The notion of Takaful can be translated as "a group of people who insure each other", the participants pool their participation and voluntary contributions and insure each other.

This tradition of guaranteeing each other is rooted in the early days of Islam in the holy book "al Qor'an" and is reflected in a multitude of Hadiths*:

► Surat Al Maida (5) verse (2) "Help each other in doing good deeds and piety and do not help each other in sin and transgression"

▶ The Prophet (saw) said, "The believers among themselves are like a building whose elements strengthen each other. Reported by Bukhari and Muslim.

According to Abu Hurairah, the Prophet (saw) said: *"Whoever has lightened the affliction of a believer in this world, God will lighten his affliction on the Day of Judgment. Whoever helps a man in trouble, God will help him in this world and in the next. Whoever covers the faults of a Muslim, God will cover them for him in this world and the next. God helps His servant as long as he helps his brother. Whoever walks the path of knowledge, God will make the path to Paradise smooth for him. As long as men gather in some house dedicated to God to recite the Qur'an and to study it together, peace of heart will descend upon them, mercy will cover them, angels will surround them and God will mention them as His own. As for the one whose deeds have put him behind, he will not be put ahead by his lineage".*

Takaful insurance is therefore a mutual guarantee, based on the principles of Islamic finance which are :

- Risk sharing between the parties to the contract;

- Materiality: any transaction must have a "material purpose", directly or indirectly linked to the real economic transaction;

- Non-exploitation and balance: financial transactions must never result in the exploitation of one of the contracting parties;

- The prohibition of financing products or activities qualified as illicit, such as the production of alcoholic beverages, pork, pornography, gambling, weapons...

Takaful is based on five fundamental elements:

i.  A mutual guarantee: creation of a solidarity fund or a mutual guarantee based on the principle of mutual aid and risk sharing between participants.

ii.  The fund is owned by the "participants": the "participants" own the solidarity fund. This fund is totally independent of the assets of the insurance company, i.e. the Takaful operator.

iii.    Rejection of uncertainty: the element of uncertainty does not come into play because the fund is fed by a donation or a voluntary contribution by the "participants" with the aim of righteousness and virtue.

iv.    The Fund Management Model: The management of the Takaful fund is not free but must follow one of the following models: Mudaraba, Wakala, Waqf... Furthermore, the supervision of the funds is carried out by an internal and external Sharia Board.

v.    Investment conditions: they must be in conformity with the Sharia. The fund must therefore be invested exclusively in "Halal" assets. The only investments allowed are those whose remuneration results from a sharing of the lot between the investors and the beneficiaries.

These principles derive from the prohibition of three practices:

•    Riba: literally increase, addition. It is in fact usury, the interest earned on money lent, borrowed or deposited in a bank account. As a reminder, one of the axioms of Islamic finance is that money is a measure of value, not a value in itself. It is the real economy that takes precedence; notional inflation is not desirable. Money does not create money.

•    Gharar: refers to any sale that is random or has an imprecise, ambiguous, uncertain, hidden or event-dependent element. The example that is often given is selling an unborn animal in its mother's womb, fish in the water or birds in the sky.

•    Maysir: any easy way to make money without work or effort, where chance is part of the equation. Example: gambling, speculation.

The principles of operation:

One of the fundamental principles is the separation of funds between the participant's fund(s) and the funds (accounts) of the Takaful operator who manages the funds.

- On the one hand, there are the participant funds or accounts that collect and receive the dividends and contributions (premiums) of the participants and pay the claims. At the end of each financial year, the surplus or excesses outside the technical provisions are redistributed to the participants.

- On the other hand, the operator or manager of the funds provides the capital necessary for the creation and solvency of the Takaful company and manages the activity on a daily basis. The eventual deficits of the funds are absorbed by the operator in return for an interest-free advance (credit) called "Kard Hassan" repayable by the funds.

The operator's management fee or remuneration, which is intended to cover its costs of managing Takaful funds and accounts, is based on the following models:

1) Wakala" management fee, under which the company receives a commission set at a flat rate or based on a percentage of participants' contributions.

This model is similar to the mandate: This mandate is used at the time of contract subscription and investment of the funds: the Takaful operator is therefore mandated by the participants to manage the funds but does not participate directly in the risk carried by the fund. All risks are borne by the fund and the surplus from the operation belongs to the participants.

This remuneration may include a performance fee which will be deducted from any surplus provided by efficient fund management.

2) Mudharaba" management fee, whereby the company receives a share of the income generated by the investments allocated to the fixed Takaful funds, as a percentage of the income generated by these investments.

The Takaful operator acts as a Mudarib (entrepreneur) and the participants are rab ul maal (capital providers). The contract specifies how the gains generated by the investment(s) will be divided between the Mudarib and the participants. Losses are also borne by the participants unless the Mudarib is guilty of malpractice or negligence, in which case he will not be entitled to his remuneration.

This remuneration may also include a performance fee which will be deducted from any surplus provided by efficient fund management.

3)     The management remuneration can also result from the combination of the management remuneration "Wakala" and "Moudharaba".

This association allows the use of the Wakala model at the time of subscription and the Mudaraba contract for the investment of Takaful funds.

This is the method most commonly used in practice by Takaful insurance companies. The operator receives a pre-determined proportional share of the contributions paid by the policyholders, and then a share of the capital gains generated by the investment activities.

Some financial regulators and international organizations recommend the hybrid model because it takes advantage of the strengths of both models.

These three models are the most common. In addition, there is a fourth model, the Wakf model. In this model, an initial contribution is made by the operator, and additional contributions are made by the insured, which are then used to settle claims. The operator has a fixed remuneration, the surplus is returned to the funds.


### 1.1.3.  THE EVOLUTION OF TAKAFUL:

The Takaful market in the world is modest but promising, it weighs 1% of the world insurance market but it shows a double digit growth rate every year.

It is interesting to note that "the forecast of $7.5 billion for 2015 established in 1999 was exceeded in 2010. In fact, according to Ernst & Young, the market at that time was already $8.3 billion, having grown by 19% compared to 2009 .*

According to the "Global Takaful Report 2017" published in July 2017 by "Milliman

---

* By EZZEDINE GHLAMALLAH (2014) "The extraordinary growth of takaful."

reseach report", the growth rate of Takaful in 2015 was 14%, see table below :

MARKET TRENDS

The performance of the general and family Takaful industries is shown below:

| SECTOR | MARKET SHARE | ESTIMATED REVENUES | GROWTH RATE IN 20IS |
|---|---|---|---|
| General Takaful | 83% | US$ 123 bn | 17% |
| Family Takaful | 17% | US$2.6 bn | (1)%- |
| Totali Takaful | 100% | US$ 14.9 bn | 14% |

Source: MIKman analysis of

industry dale

More than 226 Takaful companies and 113 takaful windows operate worldwide and offer sharia-compliant products. However, this industry remains concentrated in the Middle East and South East Asian countries.

The world's insurance and reinsurance giants have been interested in this market for over a decade. Considering its potential if we take into account the demographic weight.

Indeed, the Muslim population is expected to exceed 2.6 billion people constituting 30% of the world population.

The Moroccan market will certainly not deviate from this rule as a proof of the appetite shown by the clientele at the approach of the opening to the public of the participative finance.

The Takaful industry will be an additional growth lever for the insurance sector in Morocco.

Morocco amended its insurance code during 2016 by introducing a new regulatory framework governing takaful activity. The law n°59-13 amending and supplementing the law n° 1799 on the insurance code (published in the Official Bulletin n°6501 of September 19, 2016) specifies that companies wishing to carry out takaful activity will have to create legal entities separate from traditional insurance companies.

## 1.1.4. THE POTENTIAL IN MOROCCO IN FIGURES (ESTIMATE)

With a penetration rate of 3.1%, the Moroccan insurance market has the best performance in the MENA region and the second best on the African continent.

Assuming that Takaful activity will be introduced first by financial groups with banking and insurance subsidiaries, through this distribution network, the activity will be further promoted by bancatakaful.

Participatory banks plan to have a market share of between 5% and 10% of the overall banking sector within the next five years.

Assuming a 10% share in the banking sector in general, and note that the share of bancassurance distribution in volume is about 7 billion dirhams in 2015 with a sustained growth of 15% per year or an estimated turnover in 2018 of 8.4 billion dirhams. By applying the 10% share desired by participatory banks, bankatakaful will have a volume of 1.2 billion dirhams in 2022.

Bancassurance 2015 revenues in 7 000 000

MMAD                    15%

Tx Evol 2015/2014

| | 2018 | 2019 | 2020 | 2021 | 2022 |
|---|---|---|---|---|---|
| Tx Evolution of Bancassurance revenues | 20% | 10% | 10% | 10% | 10% |
| CA Bancassurance | 8 400 000 | 9 240 000 | 10 164 000 | 11 180 400 | 12 298 440 |
| Part Bancatakaful | 2,0% | 4% | 5% | 7% | 10% |
| CA Bancatakaful Estimated | 168 000 | 369 600 | 508200 | 782628 | 1 229844 |

Source: Bancassurance Activity Report 2015 of the Insurance and Social Prevention Supervisory Authority (ACAPS)

We can add to this potential, the turnover that could be drained by two other distribution networks:

▶ Microfinance companies and associations that are authorized to distribute insurance and de facto Takaful insurance. Although based on declarations, the various field studies have shown a strong appetite among this clientele for participatory financial products in general and Takaful products in particular.

▶ The so-called traditional network of general insurance agents and brokers. Naturally more active in non-life and especially motor business, this network will play a decisive role in "General Takaful".

## 1.2. INNOVATION

### 1.2.1. INNOVATION IN GENERAL

It is an idea or process that significantly changes a current situation for the better. Innovation is motivated by improving the lives of individuals and organizations.

Innovating also means achieving customer satisfaction by :

- The launch of **new products** or **services,** ipad, Wi-Fi, wind energy...

- **New modes of organization** (just-in-time, Internet sales, etc.),

- New **processes** (vacuum cooking, dehydrated food...).

Today, innovation concerns all sectors of activity. It is both a result: a new product, a new service, a new process, a new technology, a new know-how, and the process followed to achieve this result (an innovation project).

It is considered as the means to ensure the development of the company. The company innovates because it is the most efficient way to maintain its competitiveness in the face of competition. It is a major stake in the development or even the survival of companies which materializes at two levels:

1.      Physical, in view of the results, creation of new products or services,

2.      Organizational and managerial, because a company that innovates is perceived and experienced as a living company.

The change induced by an innovation can be of two types, revolutionary involving a radical change in the way of doing things or evolutionary.

Innovation activity has evolved in companies and is taking on more importance in strategic terms due to its multi-dimensional nature.

Innovation has become a major issue in modern society. By marketing new products and services or changing their production processes, companies are in direct interaction with consumers, the economic fabric and public authorities.

This situation has implied a strong requirement of the society, in its global sense, on innovation, an expectation and a requirement to solve all the difficulties and the problems that the modern society meets. And this, whatever the field, medical, agricultural, energy, industrial or financial ... it seems that the pace has accelerated in the last two centuries. Numerous advances in medicine, energy and services have been noted.

Innovation has driven humanity forward, albeit with difficulty. It is true that some innovative solutions have proven to be harmful: asbestos, GMOs, drifts in Internet communities, mortgages based on toxic assets and "subprimes", so many results of innovation processes that ultimately generate more problems than they solve. Isn't it said that the economic crisis of 2008 was caused by "financial innovation"?

But, overall, innovation brings positive changes:

► New processes bring productivity;

► New organizations require efficiency;

► New products bring customer satisfaction;

Innovation creates added value that fuels growth and leads to positive results for all players in the value chain.

## 1.2.2.  INNOVATION IN INSURANCE

Affecting all activities, insurance is at the heart of society. To adapt and follow the protection needs of the company, the insurer must know and master all the activities.

As such, he calls upon a range of disciplines in his daily work: mathematics, actuarial science, medicine, demography, physics, chemistry, economics, earth sciences, law, etc. Under competitive pressure and the continuous search for growth and profit, the insurer is subject to a major anticipation requirement which imposes continuous innovation to accompany the client (individual or company).

In terms of insurance offerings, innovations are often less visible than in other sectors, and we are not witnessing disruptive innovations. They are incremental innovations around the products and not within the product.

It should be noted that the contractual nature of the business, the weight of current contracts and their lifespan result in a marginal short-term effect of innovation on the results of insurance companies.

However, insurance professionals believe that innovation is essential to address the contraction of margins.

Today, the issues and challenges are numerous. These include: Regulation, standardization of the offer, customer volatility, technological advances, the emergence of new insurance distributors who master customer knowledge and relationships...

According to the first observatory of innovation in insurance, initiated by L'Argus de

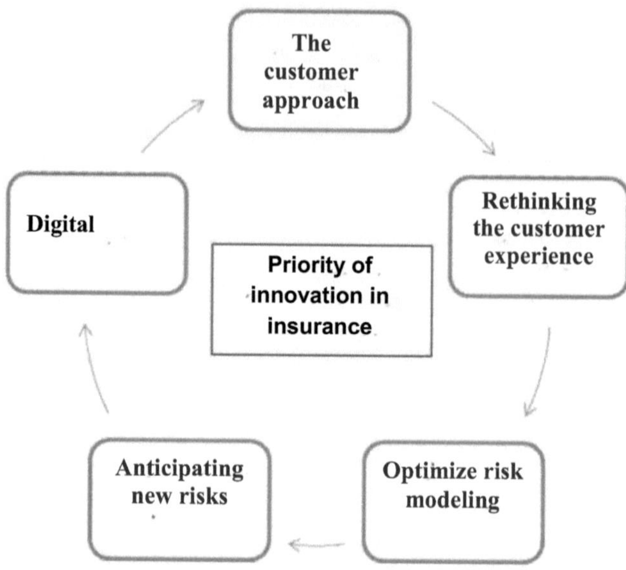


l'assurance, the Institute of Actuaries, Kurt Salmon and Opinion Way, the five priorities in terms of innovation in the insurance sector are

1. **The Client Approach:**

All insurance companies operate according to well-defined policies, practices and procedures, namely business processes.

Traditionally, insurers have been organized in silos for a long time, each carrying a branch of activity without any communication between them. The notion of "customer centricity" is new to insurance, even if it existed in the statements of the managers. The organization in silos eliminates any coherence in the marketing strategy: for example, a customer is approached by the automobile department because he is qualified as a senior (good risk) but he is not considered welcome by the health department...

Within companies, there is always a preoccupation with the technical balance per branch. Another important element in the customer approach is trust, which has been undermined in recent decades, particularly in terms of lack of transparency and information.

Having a good customer approach ultimately means responding effectively to their requirements and needs, including a competitive rate in property and casualty insurance and capital protection in life insurance, accompanied by a keen sense of listening.

2. **Rethinking the customer experience**

It comes down to answering the question, "What do today's customers want from insurance?

This is where companies can innovate more, if we take the postulate that in insurance, it is easier to make incremental innovations around products by additional services.

Beyond the product or service offered, there are many opportunities to innovate and make the customer experience pleasant: the points of contact with the customer, distribution networks, pre- and post-sales assistance, after-sales service (repair, compensation), ongoing communication, information exchange, listening.

## 3. Risk modeling

In the field of risk modelling, innovation is ongoing and tends towards better control of the models allowing the proposal of optimal coverage.

In both property and casualty and life insurance, the models have undergone a continuous transformation. This is mainly due to the emergence of new risks, the abundance of data and information, and the use of new technologies, which have made it possible to "stress" and challenge traditional models in order to obtain the most accurate evaluation and estimation possible: the integration of climate change, for example, or fluctuations in the financial markets, or the behavioral information of individuals.

However, innovations in modeling have been hampered in insurance and life reinsurance, particularly in terms of regulations and fears about hyper-segmentation that goes beyond the traditional criteria of man-woman, young-adult, smoker-non-smoker, with new criteria such as body mass index, lifestyle...

## 4. The new risks

This is the most fertile ground in terms of innovations where the limits of insurability can be pushed back. The losses recorded in the event of the realization of these risks amply exceed the damages and losses known until now.

Many risks are emerging. They are environmental, technological, geopolitical, economic and legal in nature.

These risks can concern a community of people as well as a given individual. It is the case in particular of the climatic risks, the natural disasters, the environmental risks, the cyber-attacks or the cybercriminality, the pandemics, the vehicles without drivers, the usurpation of the identity, the old age, the dependence,.

## 5. Digital

Like the various industrial changes and revolutions, the digital revolution is shaking up the historical players in all fields. The financial world is not immune. For the past decade, it has continued to suffer the effects of digitalization.

The stakes are high and will lead to the transformation of the insured-insurer relationship. It becomes essential to be vigilant on three levels:

▶ Keeping pace with the evolution of digital usage by the customer who is becoming multi-equipped in media (Smartphone, tablet, connected objects...) and adept at the principle: any time, anywhere, any device.

▶ Mastering new data technologies and answering the question of how to acquire, analyze, store and use megadata (Big data)

▶ Protect yourself from competition from new players such as GAFA (Google, Apple, Facebook and Amazon) or startups like instechs and others.

It is a mix of several factors of a technological, regulatory, consumer mode and consumer expectations nature that places digital at the center of all insurance related topics.

In short, innovation is a strategic issue for the insurance industry.

For a long time, insurers have been accused of having a "far from customer" posture, since the relationship with the latter is limited to two key moments: the purchase and the claim declaration, but they are increasingly using their ingenuity to get to know the customer better. To do so, they are multiplying contact opportunities, improving their operational efficiency and demonstrating greater agility in bringing to market new products and services that meet the needs of a new type of customer in a competitive and constantly changing environment.

# Part II: INNOVATION IN TAKAFUL

Based on the premise that Takaful itself is an innovation in contemporary insurance, we can hope that it will help to further energize the insurance sector by making innovation its DNA as an emerging industry.

In Morocco, Takaful companies, even though most will be subsidiaries of established financial groups (banks & insurance), will have to adopt a continuous innovation approach. An approach that will have to challenge the old processes, reflexes and tools that conventional companies implement on a daily basis.

Certainly, the insurance sector in Morocco has been moving in the direction of innovation and creativity over the last decade. Will the advent of Takaful accelerate this momentum? It is at least an opportunity for Moroccan insurers, through these new entities dedicated to Takaful, to test in real life and on light structures, a way of practicing insurance differently within the framework of an approach based on innovation.

## 2.1. INNOVATION IN TAKAFUL

The Islamic economy, despite its recent history, has already demonstrated its ability to serve as a resilient financial and investment system that offers a balanced approach to wealth creation, growth and distribution.

The demographic weight of youth in the Muslim world suggests significant growth opportunities for financial services and risk protection schemes.

Assuming we limit ourselves to life insurance products, and if we look at Takaful through the prism of wealth management tools, the possibilities for product innovation are multiple and will attract a very broad clientele ranging from the very wealthy to small savers looking for safety nets. The latter are relatively excluded from the financial system for reasons of conviction or purchasing power.

Not to mention designing better long-term retirement plans, waqf and inheritance and estate management for high-income individuals.

Investors targeted by takaful activity already demand more sophisticated savings, retirement, insurance and mutual fund products. They want to diversify their investments into a range of alternative products with acceptable income.

So many opportunities to innovate in terms of products and services.

## 2.1.2 INNOVATION OF SHARED ETHICAL FOUNDATIONS

Innovation strategy is paramount for the insurance sector in general and the Takaful sector is no exception.

Especially since the strategy and culture of innovation shares the ethical and even religious foundations of Takaful, three of which are mentioned:

1.    **Risk-taking**: Innovation means taking risks. Risk taking is not forbidden in Islam, on the contrary, it is even encouraged cf the hadih "Al rhounm bi al rhourm". It is to allow to experiment, to test and to allow researchers (collaborators) to be flexible to make mistakes (Mujtahid's principle) and to experiment with possible ideas, processes and solutions We can afford to adopt a "test and learn" strategy, are we not at the beginning of the genesis of an industry?

2.    **Transparency and vision sharing**: In a winning strategy, goals are clearly articulated and communicated to all stakeholders (policyholders and employees) so that the community can engage. This is a common fundamental principle, Takaful is based on transparency in terms of commitment, management and sharing. There is no innovation without commitment and shared vision.

3.    **Sharing the benefits**: Another fundamental principle is to share the purpose of this strategy. That is, policyholder satisfaction, system sustainability and employee fulfillment. Transparency in the company's reward system is essential for employees as well as in the sharing of surpluses for participants.

## 4.   1.3.   INNOVATION AND IJTIHAD

Finally, innovation and research are encouraged in all fields by the religion. Referring to the notion of "Ijtihad" which goes beyond its strict legal use in fiqh to be any effort to explore, interpret or find solutions to problems that a member of the community may face, and this in accordance with the percepts of the sharia. Moreover, the hadith in the two authentic corpora of Bukhari and Muslim is quoted in this regard: "When a person makes intellectual effort and reaches the right result, he is doubly rewarded, and if he does not reach it, he is still rewarded for his effort.

## 2.2. TYPOLOGY AND INNOVATION PATHS

## 2.2.1.  PRODUCT INNOVATION

The right objective for a Takaful company is to have a multi-dimensional approach to innovation and not just a product focus.

This multi-dimensional approach will not spare managers from first addressing product-related aspects.

Product innovation will be about intelligently evolving and perfecting the products offered by conventional insurance to bring new Shariah-compliant products and services to the market.

It is clear that at the beginning, it is imperative to meet the needs of customers, especially banks, in terms of so-called "basic" life insurance and investment products: death cover linked to bank financing products (mourabaha or others) as well as certain damage products (multi-risk housing, theft and loss of means of payment, health and hospitalization...).

In sum, Takaful companies will offer almost all types of products available on a conventional basis.

Benchmarking conventional insurance is an essential step in the development of Islamic products. It is considered the simplest strategy as the target and needs are already known.

"Imitation can help especially in the embryonic stage of Islamic finance" (Al-Suwailem, 2006).

However, it will be necessary to move quickly from imitation to mutation and then to an engineering based on the satisfaction of the needs expressed by the participants.

For the absence of a well-defined systematic innovation management process within Takaful operators at the outset will be one of the biggest challenges for the development of new products and services.

In addition, there is a need for ingenuity in various areas:

**i. Investment (savings):**

In order to boost the savings dynamic, and with the objective of financial inclusion of the population that has been excluded until now, it is necessary to innovate in terms of savings products (investment) with specific attractions:

- To small savers. By eliminating the two brakes: conviction and financial capacity.

Innovation at this stage should be understood beyond the marketing aspect of presentation and communication. It is not the savings earmarked for Haj, marriage or other that is targeted. As an example, explore new forms of tontines with low contributions.

- High-income individuals who are looking for better long-term retirement plans, especially for professionals, as they do not have pension coverage, and for inheritance and waqf management.

**ii. Death:**

Beyond the strict coverage, which is an important and necessary source at the beginning, especially to accompany the participative banks in their offers, it is to make the effort to combine prevention and certain Muslim rites.

An example is the Haj rite which is one of the five pillars of Islam and especially the concept of "Badal Al haj" where someone else performs the Haj rites on behalf of the participant (policyholder).

In the event of the participant's death or total permanent disability, a portion of the benefit is used to fund the completion of Haj Badal. This ensures that participants will not be financially disadvantaged in fulfilling any of their obligations to one of the five pillars of Islam.

### iii.  Other covers :

Other illustrative examples can be applied to either the health sector, the decrease in activity for a professional or the loss of his or her job using the conceptual advantages linked to cultural and religious aspects.

One of these products is based on provisioning in "good" years to meet hardship in "bad" years. Contributions under this policy are paid by participants for a certain number of years and benefits last for another number of deferred years.

In the case of health coverage, the contract consists of a premium payment today for coverage deferred in time from a certain age or upon retirement.

The concept refers to the Qur'an, where the king of Egypt says: "Verily, I saw (in a dream) seven coarse cows, which seven blackberries devoured - and seven green thorns and (seven) others dry".

### iv.  Micro Takaful products:

At this level, there is a significant appetite among the targeted populations but very little work has been done, with rare exceptions. It should be noted that if Takaful aims at the ultimate goal of financial inclusion and the extension of coverage to parts of the population that have been excluded from the system for various reasons: religious beliefs, purchasing power or others, we have a potential in micro Takaful to explore and exploit.

It should be noted that the examples cited are, at first sight, of interest to individuals; this is justified by the desire to benefit from the good dynamics due :

- the good penetration of the insurance concept in general in Morocco compared to other countries in the region.

- to the performance of bancassurance as a distribution model. To be replicated on the bancatakaful.

Knowing that an effort of accompaniment and innovation products will have to answer the needs of the companies and especially the small and medium ones as well as the very small.

This niche remains almost untouched as Takaful experiences around the world have been more interested in large industries.

## 2.2.2. INSTITUTIONAL ORGANIZATIONAL INNOVATION

Overall in Islamic finance, this type of innovation relates to changes in the structure of financial organizations, the creation of new types of financial intermediaries, changes in business practices and in the organization of work.

Also included in this category are changes to the supervisory framework, sharia compliance, financing framework and market regulation.

For Takaful companies, this translates into three poles:

► Innovation in the **participant fund management model**.

If the management models mentioned on page 12 (Wakala, Moudaraba, Hybrid, Waqf...), which allow the Takaful operator to be remunerated, are known and tested in other countries, in Morocco their implementation and testing is an experiment.

The companies have put forward scenarios based on assumptions. It will take a few years before each company makes the final choice of management mode. In this respect, the field of innovation in the evolutionary sense is to be explored.

▶ Takaful activity brings a new approach to **insurance company organizations**.

If "the professions" of insurance are not going to undergo radical changes, new professions and skills will have to be adapted (underwriting, investment, actuarial...) or integrate the new structures: sharia compliance...

▶ **New business and distribution models**

o Business models

The function of the Takaful operator as manager of the participants' funds implies different business models from the conventional ones. The commercial aspect is affected especially in terms of remuneration and acquisition costs.

This observation is pushing operators to innovate in terms of distribution networks and models for their remuneration.

Indeed, it has been observed that the evolution of Takaful has strongly contributed to the growth of bancassurance. In the GCC (The Cooperation Council for the Arab States of the Gulf), it has been the most effective means of distribution, especially for Family Takaful. The concept of Bancatakaful was born.

It is estimated that over 80% of Family Takaful's retail business is generated through this channel. There are other distribution channels based on small cooperatives and associations. These are best suited for micro-takaful serving the disadvantaged segments of society.

In the case of Morocco, the tradition of bancassurance is already established; bancatakaful will certainly follow suit. The innovation will concern the creation of new distribution modes or the evolution of old modes.

One of the models to encourage is the prescribers, beyond the regulatory problem of the presentation of insurance (book IV of the insurance code), takaful lends itself more.

o Distribution models

Another major challenge for Takaful is to establish a good distribution channel allocation model.

It is indeed important to know which are the preferred contact points of each participant in order to build a real circuit leading to a good customer experience.

Behavioral studies are lacking at this level for the target population of Takaful products. One can only stress the importance of this issue related to interaction with the participating policyholder, especially at the launch of Takaful, regardless of the channel:

- The agency (the intermediary or bank)

- the web

- the mobile

- social networks

- the telephone.

So many channels to master in order to respond effectively to demand. This means excelling in the multi-channel approach. We recommend adopting the omnical approach.

Omnichannelity, a new concept that is increasingly being applied by some banks abroad, is the ability for a customer to enter into a relationship, or to be contacted, with the same quality of service and continuity of management of his or her file, regardless of the channel used. This concept replaces the notion of multi-channel.

To make this omnichannel reality, it is important to put the customer at the center of our thinking about the products and services that are intended for them. This requires a detailed analysis of their uses and practices.

In some cases, the customer will want to act autonomously and will turn to the web or a mobile application; in other cases, they will want support or advice, and will choose the point of sale or the telephone. The key to this relationship is to be agile by recognizing the customer, his needs, his coverage and his contracts through any channel and at any time.

It is notably through this innovative approach that marketing actions of sales awareness can prove to be a powerful acquisition lever for new insurers and Takaful operators, whose (insurance) sector suffers from a "very serious" or even old-fashioned image, especially among young people.

The advantage is also to maintain contact with the participant through all channels. Insurers are generally blamed for the fact that they rarely contact their clients? at most twice, at the time of subscription and possibly at the time of a claim.

However, it has been shown that frequent contact with the customer gives more proximity which inevitably results in a better knowledge of the customer (case of the bank).

Aside from the benefits of omnichannel, there are two arguments that support the growth of the Takaful industry:

i.    For the client: freedom and intimacy, because it is a conviction specific to the individual who sometimes does not wish to display (be seen in an agency). He is in discovery mode. The web or telephone channel is preferred in this case.

ii.   For the Takaful operator: through the two above-mentioned channels, it ensures :

a.    standardization of the message, the terminology used and the description of the product or service being questioned. This is especially important at the start of the business.

b.    A tool to collect and store information on the prospect or customer for a better knowledge of the latter. This information can be used later in the relationship without any repetition effort by the customer.

And this is where another notion enters the customer approach introduced by omnichannel: "phygitalization.

Behind the term phygital, which combines physical and digital, lies a complex machinery: that of data management.

The operator must be able to process information very quickly and make it available to all channels in order to know the customer and serve him. It is also a new method of information management.

Insurance companies in Morocco are struggling to implement this kind of approach, the creation of a Takaful subsidiary is an opportunity for its implementation.

## 2.2.3.  TECHNOLOGICAL INNOVATION

These innovations involve the introduction of new processes or technologies leading to greater efficiency. When we talk about technology in insurance, data is always the central topic: how to acquire it, dematerialize it, analyze it, store it, secure it, use it.

Without getting into the debate, which sometimes discourages large institutions from making the effort to transform themselves, we cite below the major families of technological innovations that have already begun to have a strong impact on the insurance sector:

i.     Big Data refers to a set of technological tools that enable the production of new knowledge and solutions from the collection of big data produced through digital businesses. It is a set of data that becomes so voluminous that it becomes difficult - if not impossible - to work with traditional tools.

ii.     The Internet of Things ("IoT"), which refers to all objects in the real world that allow for the exchange of information and data to the Internet: (wristbands, watches, smartphones, refrigerators, cars, etc.)

iii.     Artificial intelligence: A.I. provides considerable assistance in the analysis of claims, situations of difficulty and therefore upstream an efficient calculation of premiums and drafting of contracts. The use of A.I. facilitates the analysis of accidents, disasters and damage caused.

The pace of innovation in companies is increasing. Almost all companies are reinventing all or part of their core activities to keep pace with changes in society and in people's behavior.

In a highly regulated environment with stringent requirements in terms of security and data quality, the adoption of new technologies will introduce more rigor and rationality in some of the activities of insurers.

New information technologies (digital) should not be understood by Takaful operators as mere means (channels) of communication but as an opportunity to combine all channels in order to federate an approach that includes the business (manager-insurance), the customer relationship (marketing-communication) and the distribution (commercial) at the service of the participants.

Especially as media and social networks become more important. They are proliferating rapidly because people, regardless of their age, education level and purchasing power, are equipped with more computers, laptops and mobile devices (tablets and smartphones).

These tools are widely connected to the Internet, which allows for instantaneous information sharing and communication.

The rate of equipment in support (device) and connectivity to the Internet is quite edifying, Morocco is no exception.

The McKinsey firm in its report on social technologies[†] indicates that companies are increasingly adopting social networks to "increase agility and manage organizational complexity." A range of technologies are deployed by 86% of respondents in high-tech and telecommunications companies, 62% of energy companies and 64% of financial services. The measurable benefits cited are: "access to knowledge", "increased organizational efficiency", "reduced communication and travel costs" and "access to external experts".

Takaful needs to "catch the wave" and embrace the movement in a more pronounced way than conventional insurance companies. The latter are struggling to make their digital transformation and their approach is tainted with hesitation.

By seizing this opportunity and joining forces with the new fintech startup operators, especially the instechs, Takaful operators will be able to better negotiate this shift and accompany these evolutions.

It is recommended that takaful operators:

• Use digital tools as an essential component in a phygital distribution network vision by adopting a digitalized relational model with the customer. This model increases the availability and the active listening of the Takaful operator towards his customer.

Another way to deploy massively and reach the maximum number of prospects and customers.

---

[†] "McKinsey: The social economy " unlocking value and productivity through social

- Optimize the presence on social media. It is the most impactful relationship relay with a competitive cost. Especially when the target population is equipped (tools and internet connectivity). Social media is a good channel to inform, recruit and serve the target population.

Essentially, customers will be invited to be part of the company's internal product exchange, make suggestions on new products, file claims that other community members can view, as well as have real-time access to their own accounts for updating personal information or tracking claims.

- Integrate startups or other fintechs in the innovation process, the Takaful operator will act either as an incubator or as a privileged partner. In a co-construction process, fintechs can act as gas pedals and sources of ideas for the operators. The relationship with these startups is balanced since on the one hand the fintechs bring ideas, solutions and implementation agility, while on the Takaful operator's side, it is the insurer's business (technicality) with access to the different markets in compliance with the regulations in force.

# Part III: CHALLENGES AND LIMITATIONS FOR INNOVATION IN TAKAFUL

## 3.1. HUMAN CAPITAL

Innovation in Takaful brings new ways of working and induces a strong cultural and organizational change.

The first challenge is to identify the human resources that will carry the Takaful projects and feed this innovation dynamic on a daily basis. It is a question of identifying and accompanying the dedicated skills in order to instill the new approach to insurance practice.

This problem, encountered by participatory banks, is acknowledged for Takaful. Takaful will face a problem of scarcity of skills at the beginning.

Addressing the potential lack of appropriate human resources (actuaries, marketers, information systems, finance, new technologies...) will significantly help the business to evolve.

## 3.2. CUSTOMER EXPECTATIONS

Like any new entrant in a market, the Takaful operator will be expected to provide a high quality of service. Today, policyholders are accustomed to a level of service quality, care, speed of compensation, return on investment, which must be maintained or even surpassed to make a difference in view of the high expectations.

Moreover, initially Takaful operators will have to manage the divergence between clients' expectations and their perceptions of the service provided. Indeed, as customers' financial awareness increases, they have high expectations for high quality service.

## 3.3. THE DOUBLE BURDEN OF REGULATION

We remind you that unlike conventional finance, the success of Islamic finance depends on both faith and economics.

Therefore, in addition to the regulatory filter for "approval" of products and services, there is also the filter of Sharia compliance. This impacts the "Time to Market" which could be higher than that of conventional products.

Flexible regulatory frameworks are desirable, particularly with respect to technological innovation.

# CONCLUSIONS:

Takaful as a segment of participatory finance reflects the ethical aspirations and investments in tangible economic activities of a segment of the Moroccan population.

Following the example of other countries, this "participative", mutualist, socially responsible and not exclusively communitarian insurance will certainly grow in our country. Taking advantage of the creation of new entities, Takaful operators would gain by daring to create light structures that are customer-oriented, innovative, digitalized and open to external startups and instechs.

The objective for Takaful should be to approach the innovation activity in a multi-dimensional way and not only focused on the product:

- New ways to subscribe and produce

- New networks, partners and prescribers

- New pricing strategies

- New product offerings

- New business models

- Best customer experiences.

Beyond the religious aspect, it is essential for Takaful companies to maintain trust and transparency by reassuring and informing. This translates into accompanying the client from the signing of the contract to its completion, thinking globally about the client's coverage needs and advising him in his choices and decisions.

However, Takaful will have to overcome obstacles that could hinder its growth. These include a scarcity of skills, low public awareness (inherited from conventional insurance) and a double burden of regulation and sharia.

# APPENDICES

## TAKAFUL

## Overview of the regulatory framework
## in Morocco

### 1.1   The regulatory framework of participatory finance in Morocco

In Morocco, participatory finance benefits from an appropriate regulatory framework by adapting the laws relating to the three main components of the ecosystem, namely participatory banks, Takaful insurance and the financial market, while respecting the Shari'a opinion of the Supreme Council of Oulémas CSO.

For banks, the law n° 103.12 relating to credit institutions and similar bodies introduces participative banks in the banking code through the establishment of new foundations.

The text sets out the regulatory framework for the creation, operation and activities of participatory banks and defines the points concerning the field of application, deposits and products marketed by participatory banks. The regulatory body of this activity is Bank Al-Maghrib (BAM).

The law relating to Takaful insurance is in the form of additional articles forming part of the insurance code. Law 59-13 amending and supplementing Law No. 17-99 on the insurance code and establishing Takaful insurance in Morocco was published in the Official Bulletin No. 6501 of September 19, 2016. The regulatory body for Takaful insurance is the Autorité de Contrôle des Assurances et de Prévoyance Sociale (ACAPS).

For the Financial Market, the new financial instruments Sukuks certificates were introduced in 2013 at the level of the securitization law. The regulatory body of the financial market is the Moroccan Capital Market Authority (AMMC).

## 1.2    The regulatory framework of Takaful insurance in Morocco

Apart from the specificities of Takaful Insurance specified in this law, future Takaful operators will be subject to the same insurance code as conventional insurance companies.

The drafts of the decree and the explanatory circular of the application of the law, were communicated by ACAPS on 12/06/17, Below is the census of the different current regulatory sources governing Takaful insurance in Morocco:

► The decree of the Minister of Finance and Privatization n°1548-05 of Ramadan 1426 (October 10, 2005) relating to insurance and reinsurance companies.

► Law 59-13 amending and supplementing Law 17-99 on the insurance code

► Law n° 17-99 on the insurance code promulgated by dahir n° 1-02-238 of 25 rejeb 1423 (October 3, 2002), as amended and completed, in particular its articles 10-5, 248 and 248-1.

► The draft circular of the Insurance and Social Security Supervisory Authority setting out the specific provisions relating to Takaful insurance

► The draft order of the Minister of Economy and Finance on Takaful insurance

► The drafts of the decree of the standard general conditions of the Takaful insurance contracts for the contracts Death Borrower, Multirisk Building and Savings

## 1.3. Regulatory particularities of Takaful in Morocco

- Article 1 defines Takaful Insurance as follows "*Takaful insurance: Insurance operation carried out in accordance with the approved opinions of the Higher Council of Ulema provided for in Dahir n° 1-03-300 of Rabii I 2, 1425 (April 22, 2004) relating to the reorganization of the Councils of Ulema having as object the coverage of the risks provided for in the Takaful insurance contract by a Takaful insurance account managed, in return for a management fee, by an insurance and reinsurance company approved to carry out Takaful insurance operations Takaful insurance operations and the activity of management of the Takaful insurance account by an insurance and reinsurance company may not, under any circumstances, give rise to the collection or payment of interest.*

- The separation of life and non-life approvals, which obliges Takaful operators to create two separate legal structures Family and General with a minimum capital of 50 MDH for each company.

- The Shariah compliance of Takaful insurance operations is pronounced by the Shariah Committee for Finance, established within the Supreme Council of Ulema. "The Shariah compliance of Takaful insurance operations is pronounced by the Supreme Council of Ulema through the Committee for Participatory Finance (Art. 10-1).

- Assumption of risk by the participants' community within the limit of their contribution to the Takaful insurance account; (Art. 10-2)

- Exemption of Takaful insurance operations from any payment or collection of interest; (Art. 1)

- Management of Takaful insurance in return for a remuneration, the amount and method of which are fixed by the Administration; (Art. 1)

- Keep and manage Takaful accounts separately from its own accounts; (Art. 10-2)

- The Takaful insurance contract must specify, in addition to the information required in any insurance contract: (Art. 12) The methods of remuneration of the insurance company; the distribution of technical and financial surpluses among the participants; the conditions relating to the investments of the insurance company.

- In the event of a shortfall in the assets representing the technical provisions in relation to the said provisions, the insurance and reinsurance company must make up the shortfall by means of Takaful advances, under the conditions laid down by regulation. This provision must be stated in every Takaful insurance contract (Article 10-3);

- The technical and financial surpluses realized are distributed in full to the participants after deduction, where applicable, of Takaful advances and constitution of provisions and reserves (art. 10-3);

- <sup>ère</sup>Specimen Takaful contracts can only be issued for the first time after the approval of the authority and the opinion of the Higher Council of Ulema (Art. 247)

- Reinsurance of risks covered by Takaful contracts must be carried out with insurance companies licensed to carry out Takaful insurance. However, the law makes an exception to this principle by introducing the possibility of reinsurance with other insurers in case of absence or insufficiency of reinsurance offers (art. 247). The rules for reinsurance are set out in a Circular of the Authority.

- The Takaful reinsurance treaty must specify

- The general and special conditions of Takaful reinsurance;

- The terms of remuneration of the company as well as those relating to the distribution of technical and financial surpluses between the various reinsurance companies;

- Conditions for financial investments.

- Article 33 and 34: Requisition ^ Retained premium does not bear interest ;

- Article 100: Takaful insurance shall not provide for profit sharing;

- Article 165: The exclusivity of the Takaful insurance license;

- Article 239-2: Internal control system and internal audit structure: risk of non-compliance with CSO opinions with a specific report;

- Article 248-1: The administration may determine the methods of remuneration for the management of Takaful insurance as well as the methods of distribution of surpluses.

# BIBLIOGRAPHY :

- Sandrine Fernez-Walch & François Romon *Le Management de l'innovation, De la stratégie aux projets*. 3rd edition, Vuibert.

- Insurance white paper 2*: Innovation in insurance. Restitution of the work of the finance innovation cluster*: French Federation of Insurance Companies. 2013.

- Eurogroup consulting "*Innovation/Disruption risk or opportunity for the insurance industry*" September 2016

- Bain & Company: *Digitalization in insurance: "The multibillion dollar opportunity"*. March 20, 2017. By Henrik Naujoks, Florian Mueller and Nikos Kotalakidis.

- Lanrent Calmed "Succeeding in the digital transformation of the insurance company. Essentials. September 2016

- By EZZEDINE GHLAMALLAH (2014) "The extraordinary growth of takaful" L'argus de l'assurance.

- *The Argus of Insurance. N° 7294 - December 14, 2012. Argusdelassurance.com*

- Adeel Mushtaq (Published April 19, 2017) "Will *insurtech disrupt or complement Takaful?* "linkedin.

- Bancassurance Activity Report (2015) of the Insurance and Social Prevention Supervisory Authority (ACAPS).

- Atlas-mag.net/article/insurance-takaful

Printed by Books on Demand GmbH, Norderstedt / Germany